To Anne, Nancy, Penn, Tina, and Aly

Environmental impact statement

Rainforests is printed on-demand, meaning books are only produced as they are ordered, which reduces excess production and waste. *Rainforests* is printed on acid-free paper stock supplied by an FSC-certified provider. In order to reduce its ecological footprint, *Rainforests* does not use glossy paper for interior pages.

At the end of each year, Mongabay.com attempts to quantify all greenhouse gas emissions associated with operations, including server and bandwidth use, travel, equipment purchases, and materials use and production. Mongabay then offsets a minimum of twice this emissions estimate by supporting an effort to conserve tropical forests in Colombia's Darien region. The initiative is run by Anthrotect, an organization that works with Afro-indigenous and Embera communities to protect forests and develop sustainable livelihoods in an area that was until recently beset by conflict and violence.

Pico Bonito rainforest in Honduras

CONTENTS

Above: Rainforest in Danum Valley, in Sabah, a state in Malaysian Borneo.

My paradise looks like this picture. It is a rainforest in Borneo, a place full of orangutans, hornbills, leaf monkeys, and jawdropping kinds of insects. My moments in this forest have been among my most precious—hiking under the giant trees, swimming in the crystal clear creeks, and watching the animals.

But this place no longer exists. After my last visit, when I was 17, a logging company chopped down the trees and bulldozed the creeks. I don't know what happened to the animals.

But in this forest's destruction, something else was born: a person impassioned and determined to make a difference.

My passion for rainforests came at an early age.

I was a lucky child: my mom was a travel agent specializing in exotic locales, and my dad had about a million frequent flyer miles. They wanted to show my sister and me the world.

So we traveled all over. We went to places like Botswana, Australia, Costa Rica, Venezuela, and of course, Borneo.

Me at various stages of my progression as a nature lover: California tidepools in the 1980s, the Smithsonian in Washington D.C. in the 1980s, the Amazon in 1999, Panama in 2011 (left to right). Facing page: Rainforest in Borneo like that which was destroyed. Middle left: Male Bornean orangutan; right: red leaf monkey.

Borneo wasn't the first special place I lost, and it certainly wasn't the last. The destruction of that particular forest, however, inspired me to try to make a difference.

In college I started writing a book to raise awareness of these places and what was happening to them. I spent three years writing the book and eventually found a publisher. Everything seemed to be going well.

Then one day I received some bad news from the publisher: it didn't have money to put pictures in the book. But how could I convey the beauty of these places without photos?

That question lingered in my mind for weeks. Then I remembered why I wrote the book in the first place. I didn't write it for money, I wrote it to make people care about rainforests.

The next day I started creating a web site so I could post the book online for free. I called the web site mongabay.com after another special place: Nosy Mangabe, a spectacular island off Madagascar.

Much to my surprise, the web site grew popular. So popular, in fact, that I thought I might try to make a living writing about rainforests. I quit my day job and never looked back. Since then mongabay.com has become one of the most popular conservation sites on the Web. The kids' section, upon which this book is based, is now available in nearly 40 languages, and I have posted more than 50,000 photos that I've taken in dozens of countries. I've had opportunities to travel the world and meet fascinating people.

Most importantly, mongabay.com has had a real impact. It has introduced the beauty of rainforests to millions of people; supported rainforest conservation efforts in several countries; and helped stop destructive projects in Africa, Indonesia, and New Guinea. My dream has turned into something bigger than I ever imagined.

I hope *Rainforests* can be an inspiration for you. Maybe your dream isn't saving rainforests, but I hope my story shows that today anyone can make a difference.

My parting message is that it's going to take people with all backgrounds and interests—writers, photographers, programmers, performers, artists—to save the planet's rainforests, but if you follow your passion, you can make a difference. Together we can save the Borneos, the Madagascars, or whatever places you call paradise.

The island of Nosy Mangabe in Madagascar: beaches, reefs, lemurs, chameleons, geckos, frogs, humpback whales, and much more. My version of paradise. What's yours?

The black-and-white ruffed lemur (top), the lowland tenrec (middle left), and the green Mantella frog (middle right) are among the animals found on Nosy Mangabe (bottom).

5

1
ABOUT RAINFORESTS

Rainforest in Borneo

Rainforest in Indonesian Borneo

On my first visit to the rainforest I was amazed by the lushness of the vegetation, the giant trees, and the hanging vines. There were so many more types of plants than in the forests near my home in California. I had never seen so many shades of green.

Since then I have made many more trips to the rainforest—more than I can count. I have also traveled to a lot of non-rainforest places: deserts in Africa, coral reefs in the South Pacific, boreal forests in Alaska, and many others. While each of these places has its own unique plants and animals, there is one constant: the unpredictability of nature. When you spend a day out in the forest or on the ocean you never know exactly what you are going to see. Maybe you'll find an unusual insect under a leaf, see a whale breach, or hear a new bird song. Whatever it is, nature always holds the promise of something new and unexpected.

I've had many surprises in my travels to the rainforest. One of the scariest took place in the rainforests of Gabon, a small coastal country in Central Africa. Gabon is famous for its wildlife, including lowland gorillas. On a hike in the forest with some rangers and a photographer we unexpectedly encountered a group of gorillas, which was led by a giant male silverback. As soon as we saw them we stopped, but it was too late—the silverback had already decided to let us know who ruled the forest. He charged, beating his chest and grunting while galloping full speed at me. The ground shook with his weight—a full grown silverback can easily weigh 350 pounds, most of which is muscle. On my knees—the recommended position if a gorilla charges—all I could do was to try to avoid conflict by averting my eyes from him and staring at the ground where the leaves bounced with his every stride. My heart raced as he barreled closer and closer. Then suddenly he stopped. His tense body relaxed, his breathing slowed, and he turned away, seeming to lose interest. The forest was again still and we crept slowly away. What had started out as a hike through the forest, turned into one of the most exhilarating moments of my life.

Facing page: Lowland silverback gorilla like the one that charged me in Gabon.

What is a rainforest?

Tropical rainforests are forests with tall trees, warm climates, and lots of rain. In some rainforests it rains more than one inch nearly every day of the year!

Where are rainforests located?

Rainforests are found in Africa, Asia, Australia, and Central and South America. The largest rainforest in the world is the Amazon rainforest in South America.

Rainforests are found in the tropics, the region between the Tropic of Cancer and the Tropic of Capricorn, just above and below the Equator. In this tropic zone the sun is very strong and shines about the same amount of time every day all year long, keeping the climate warm and relatively stable.

Many countries have tropical forests. The countries with the largest areas of tropical forest are (in order):

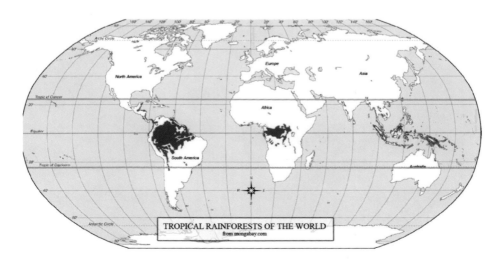

TROPICAL RAINFORESTS OF THE WORLD
from mongabay.com

- Brazil
- Democratic Republic of Congo
- Indonesia
- Peru
- Colombia

Other countries that have large areas of rainforest include Bolivia, Cameroon, Central African Republic, Ecuador, Gabon, Guyana, India, Laos, Malaysia, Mexico, Myanmar, Papua New Guinea, Republic of Congo, Suriname, and Venezuela.

Strangler fig tree in the lowland rainforest of Tangkoko National Park in North Sulawesi, Indonesia. Tangkoko is famous for tarsiers (left), one of the world's smallest primates, and the critically endangered black crested macaque (right).

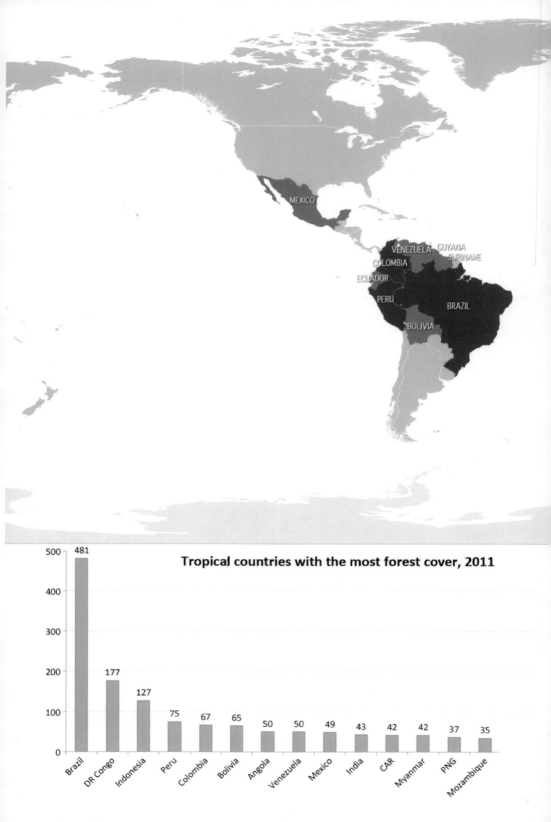

Tropical countries with the most forest cover, 2011

Country	Value
Brazil	481
DR Congo	177
Indonesia	127
Peru	75
Colombia	67
Bolivia	65
Angola	50
Venezuela	50
Mexico	49
India	43
CAR	42
Myanmar	42
PNG	37
Mozambique	35

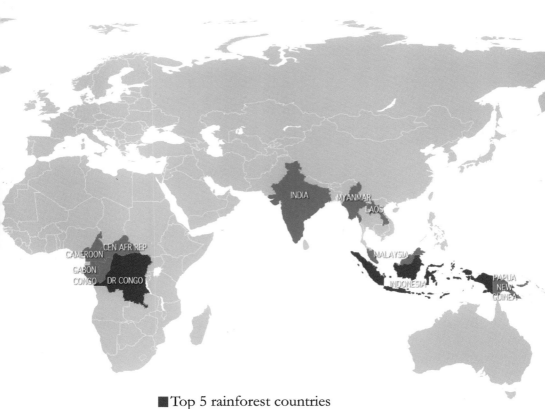

■ Top 5 rainforest countries
■ Other countries with extensive rainforests

(million hectares; forest defined as 25% tree cover)

PNG = Papua New Guinea; CAR = Central African Republic; DR Congo = Democratic Republic of Congo. Based on Saatchi et al 2011.

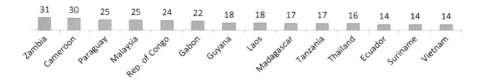

31	30	25	25	24	22	18	18	17	17	16	14	14	14
Zambia	Cameroon	Paraguay	Malaysia	Rep. of Congo	Gabon	Guyana	Laos	Madagascar	Tanzania	Thailand	Ecuador	Suriname	Vietnam

What makes a rainforest?

Each rainforest is unique, but there are certain features common to all tropical rainforests.

- Location: rainforests lie in the tropics.
- Rainfall: rainforests receive at least 80 inches (200 cm) of rain per year.
- Canopy: rainforests have a canopy, which is the layer of branches and leaves formed by closely spaced rainforest trees. Most of the plants and animals in the rainforest live in the canopy. The canopy may be 100 feet (30 m) above the ground.
- Biodiversity: rainforests have a high level of biological diversity or "biodiversity". Biodiversity is the name for all living things—like plants, animals, and fungi—found in an ecosystem. Scientists believe that about half of the plants and animals found on Earth's land surface live in rainforests.
- Symbiotic relationships between species: species in the rainforest often work together. In a symbiotic relationship, two different species benefit by helping each other—you can think of it as a partnership. For example, some plants produce small housing structures and sugar for ants. In return the ants protect the plants from other insects that want to feed on the plant's leaves.

Facing page: Giant dipterocarp tree in Gunung Leuser National Park on Sumatra island, Indonesia. Dipterocarps are commonly logged for timber.

What is the canopy?

In the rainforest most plant and animal life is not found on the forest floor, but in the leafy world known as the canopy. The canopy, which may be over 100 feet (30 m) above the ground, is made up of the overlapping branches and leaves of rainforest trees. Scientists estimate that 60-90 percent of life in the rainforest is found in the trees, making this the richest habitat for plant and animal life. Many well-known animals such as monkeys, frogs, lizards, birds, snakes, sloths, and small cats are found in the canopy.

The conditions of the canopy are very different from the conditions of the forest floor. During the day, the canopy is drier and hotter than other parts of the forest, and the plants and animals that live there are specially adapted for life in the trees. For example, because the amount of leaves in the canopy can make it difficult to see more than a few feet, many canopy animals rely on loud calls or lyrical songs for communication. Gaps between trees mean that some canopy animals fly, glide, or jump to move about in the treetops.

Scientists have long been interested in studying the canopy, but the height of trees made research difficult until recently. Today there are special facilities with rope bridges, ladders, and towers to help scientists discover the secrets of the canopy.

Rainforest canopy in Peru.

Canopy walkway near Arenal in Costa Rica and a series of ladders on Barro Colorado Island in Panama. Scientists use a wide range of tools and methods for researching the canopy, where the bulk of rainforest life is found.

Overstory

50 m

40 m

Canopy

30 m

Understory

20 m

10 m

Shrub Layer

Floor

mongabay.com

Left: Lowland rainforest in Sabah, Malaysia. Note the darkness of the forest floor due to the thickness of the canopy, which largely blocks sunlight.

18

The canopy is just one of several vertical layers in the rainforest. Take a look at the diagram on the left to see the other layers (the overstory, understory, shrub layer, and forest floor).

The rainforest floor

The rainforest floor is often dark and humid due to constant shade from the canopy's leaves. Despite its shade, the rainforest floor is an important part of the forest ecosystem.

The forest floor is where decomposition takes place. Decomposition is the process by which fungi and microorganisms break down dead plants and animals and recycle essential materials and nutrients.

Also, many of the largest rainforest animals are found on the forest floor. Some of these are elephants (in Asia), the tapir (Southeast Asia and Central and South America), tigers (Asia), and the jaguar (Central and South America).

Right: Sumatran elephants in Bukit Barisan Selatan National Park, South Sumatra, Indonesia. Human-elephant conflict is common in parts of Sumatra where people have encroached on forests typically used by elephants. The result is wild Sumatran elephants are increasingly rare.

Rainforest rivers

Due to the tremendous amount of rainfall they receive, tropical rainforests have some of the largest rivers in the world, like the Amazon, Mekong, Orinoco, and Congo. These mega-rivers are fed by countless smaller tributaries, streams, and creeks. For example, the Amazon alone has some 1,100 tributaries, 17 of which are over 1,000 miles (1,600 kilometers) long!

Top: Meandering rainforest river in West Papua, Indonesian New Guinea. Lower left: creek in Gunung Palung, Indonesian Borneo; lower right: waterfall near Arenal, Costa Rica. Facing page - top: map of rivers in the Amazon River Basin (courtesy of NASA); lower left: Angel Falls in Venezuela, which eventually flows into the Orinoco River, is fed by rainfall from the Amazon rainforest; lower right: Tad Kwang Si in Lao PDR.

2
RAINFOREST WILDLIFE

Young lowland gorilla in Gabon

The knobbed hornbill (Aceros cassidix) is found on Sulawesi and surrounding islands. Like other Indonesian hornbill species, the knobbed hornbill feeds primarily on fruit.

For me, the highlight of visiting a rainforest is seeing the animals, but spotting animals in the rainforest is very different from watching them in other parts of the world. Many rainforest animals are shy, live in the tree tops, or come out only out night. Therefore, when looking for wildlife in the rainforest you will have the most luck if you use all your senses. Listen for birds calling and monkeys jumping between trees. Pay attention to unusual smells—many rainforest animals leave "scent-marks" to mark their territory or communicate with mates and rivals. And look closely at the vegetation around you. Many rainforest animals—especially insects, amphibians, and reptiles—are experts at disguising themselves like leaves, twigs, or bark.

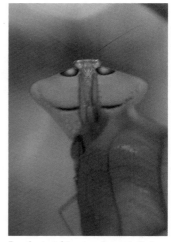

Leaf-mimicking praying mantis in Suriname

Why do rainforests have so many kinds of plants and animals?

Tropical rainforests support the greatest diversity of living organisms on Earth. Although they cover less than 2 percent of Earth's surface, rainforests house more than 50 percent of the plants and animals on Earth.

Here are some examples of the richness of rainforests:
- Rainforests have 170,000 of the world's 250,000 known plant species.
- the United States has 81 species of frogs, while Madagascar, which is smaller than Texas, may have 500 species.
- An area of rainforest the size of two football fields (one hectare) may have more than 400 species of trees, while an equal area of forest in the United States may have fewer than 20.
- Europe has 570 butterfly species, while Manu National Park, a single reserve in Peru, has 1,300 species.

Rainforests have an abundance of plants and animals for the following reasons:
- Climate: because rainforests are located in tropical regions, they receive a lot of sunlight. The sunlight is converted to energy by plants through the process of photosynthesis. Since there is a lot of sunlight, there is a lot of energy in the rainforest. This energy is stored in plant vegetation, which is eaten by animals. The abundance of energy supports an abundance of plant and animal species.
- Canopy: the canopy structure of the rainforest provides an abundance of places for plants to grow and animals to live. The canopy offers sources of food, shelter, and hiding places, providing for interaction between different species. For example, there are plants in the canopy called bromeliads that store water in their leaves. Frogs and other animals use these pockets of water for hunting and laying their eggs.

The giant monkey frog
(Phyllomedusa bicolor)
of Peru is known for its
mind-altering skin secretions.
Shamans in the Amazon
have used this species in
hunting rituals.

Malayan tiger   Scarlet macaw in Peru

It is important to note that many species in the rainforest, especially insects and fungi, have not even been discovered yet by scientists. Every year new species of mammals, birds, frogs, and reptiles are found in rainforests.

Rainforest mammals

Tropical rainforests are home to many kinds of mammals, ranging in size from tiny mouse lemurs to the African forest elephant. While large mammals like cats (tigers, jaguars, leopards, and small cats) and primates (including monkeys, apes, and lemurs) are best known, most rainforest mammals are small, nocturnal, and inconspicuous. Bats and rodents are the most abundant kinds of mammals in most rainforests.

Jaguar in Colombia

Red river hog

Three-toed sloth in Panama

Baby spectral tarsier with mother in
Tangkoko N.P., Sulawesi, Indonesia

Woolly monkey in Colombia

Male Sumatran orangutan in
Gunung Leuser N.P., Indonesia

Rainforest birds

Tropical rainforests are home to many kinds of birds, including parrots, hornbills, toucans, and raptors like eagles, hawks, and vultures.

Some migratory birds live in rainforests during the winter and return to cooler regions during the spring and summer. For example, many songbirds that nest in the United States winter in Central America or even the Amazon.

Gray-winged Trumpeters (Psophia crepitans) in Suriname

Blue-and-gold macaw (Ara ararauna) in Colombia

Harpy eagle (Harpia harpyja) in Panama

Facing page. Top: Golden-neck Cassowary (Casuarius unappendiculatus). Lower left: Macaws and other parrots feeding on clay in Peru. Clay provides macaws with minerals and helps counter dietary toxins ingested during the consumption of immature seeds. Right: Great blue turaco (Corythaeola cristata)

Rainforest reptiles & amphibians

Tropical rainforests are home to a huge diversity of reptiles (snakes, lizards, turtles, tortoises, and crocodiles) and amphibians (frogs, toads, salamanders, newts, and worm-like caecilians). These are found in virtually all rainforest habitats, ranging from the high canopy to streams and creeks. Collectively, reptiles and amphibians are known as herps.

Unfortunately, many herps are threatened by habitat loss, the pet trade, and environmental change. Amphibians are particularly at risk from a deadly disease that is spreading around the globe. The disease has already caused the extinction of at least 170 species of frogs and toads over the past 30 years. Scientists have not yet pinpointed what is causing the outbreak or how it can be controlled. Emergency measures have been implemented for some endangered species, which are being collected and kept in zoos, aquariums, and botanical gardens until a cure can be found.

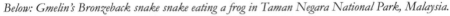

Below: Gmelin's Bronzeback snake snake eating a frog in Taman Negara National Park, Malaysia.

Red-eyed tree frog (Agalychnis callidryas) of Central America

Male panther chameleon (Furcifer pardalis) in Madagascar

Anole in Panama

Rainforest fish

Tropical rainforest waters—including rivers, creeks, lakes, and swamps—are home to the majority of freshwater fish species. The Amazon Basin alone has over 3,000 known species and possibly as many unidentified species.

Many of the tropical fish kept in freshwater aquariums are originally from the rainforest. Fish like angelfish, neon tetras, discus, and common algae-eating catfish come from the tropical forests of South America, while danios, gouramis, Siamese fighting fish (or Betta), and the clown loach are from Asia.

Altum Angelfish

Piranha in Guyana (photo by Tiffany Roufs)

South American leaf fish

Facing - top: leaf-tailed gecko in Madagascar; blue poison dart frog (Dendrobates azureus). 2nd row: tree runner lizard (Plica plica) in Colombia; Tokay gecko (Gekko gecko) in Bali, Indonesia; peacock day gecko (Phelsuma quadriocellata) in Madagascar. 3rd row: Asian vine snake (Ahaetulla prasina) in Indonesian Borneo; clown tree frog (Dendropsophus leucophyllatus) in Colombia. Bottom row: black caiman (Melanosuchus niger) in Brazil's Pantanal; emerald boa (Corallus caninus)

Rainforest invertebrates

Most of the animal species found in the rainforest are invertebrates, including insects, arachnids (such as spiders and scorpions), and worms.

Amazingly, about one quarter of all animal species that have been named and described by scientists are beetles. More than 500,000 kinds of beetles are known to exist, many of them from the world's rainforests.

Rainforest invertebrates come in an incredible array of sizes, ranging from organisms that can sit on a pinhead to the goliath beetle of Africa, which can weigh nearly a quarter of a pound (110 grams). Some Bornean stick insects—which are experts in disguise—can attain a length of more than 20 inches (50cm).

Bennett's blue weevil (Eupholus bennetti) from Indonesian New Guinea

Malay Red Harlequin (Paralaxita damajanti)

Red grasshawk in Borneo

Facing - top: planthopper nymph in Suriname; Tiger Longwing (Heliconius hecale) in Costa Rica. 2nd row: planthopper in Costa Rica; flag footed bug in Colombia; flatid leaf bugs (Phromnia rosea) in Isalo, Madagascar. 3rd row: beetle in Indonesian Borneo; beetle in Bali, Indonesia. 4th row: Curculionidae weevil in Ranomafana, Madagascar; Blushing Phantom (Cithaerias pireta) in Panama.

Color & camouflage

Because plants grow year round in the tropical rainforest, they must continuously defend themselves against many types of predators. Their defenses are usually mechanical or biochemical. Mechanical defenses include thorns, spines, and stinging hairs. Biochemical defenses include compounds that are poisonous or cause skin irritation (like poison ivy or poison oak) or make their leaves taste bad.

In response, some insects have adapted to these compounds by eating certain types of plants that normally taste bad or make other insects sick. Some of these specialist insects use such plant compounds to generate their own toxins, which in turn, make them poisonous or foul tasting to other predators.

But that's not all: the cycle sometimes continues up the food chain. For example, poison dart frogs—named because they produce toxic compounds used by rainforest people to make hunting arrows poisonous—get their poison from the insects they eat.

Poisonous animals—like dart frogs—are often colorful. Their bright colors serve as a warning to predators, telling them to stay away. It only takes one or two mistakes by a predator eating the wrong prey and getting very sick to learn to avoid a toxic species.

Many rainforest species, however, use the opposite approach: camouflage, which allows them to blend into their surroundings to avoid detection. Insects, amphibians, reptiles, birds, and even mammals—like big cats—rely on camouflage to disguise themselves from predators or to sneak up on prey.

The leaf-tailed gecko of Madagascar

Top: Malayan leaf frog in Borneo; beetle in Bali, Indonesia. 2nd row: common potoo (Nyctibius griseus), a bird, in Costa Rica; stick insect in Indonesia; Leaf-tailed gecko (uroplatus fimbriatus) on Nosy Mangabe. 3rd row: butterfly in Indonesian Borneo; leaf-mimicking katydid in Madagascar. 4th row: Leaf-like moth in Honduras; leaf-like katydid in Madagascar.

Rainforest plants

The forest floor of old-growth rainforest is rarely the thick, tangled jungle seen in movies and adventure stories. It is usually relatively clear of dense vegetation due to the deep darkness created by the canopy. So instead of choking vegetation, a visitor to the rainforest will find large tree trunks interspersed with hanging vines, countless seedlings and saplings, and a relatively small number of ground plants.

Because rainforest trees are in a constant battle for access to sunlight, they grow straight and tall, only branching near the top of their long, pole-like trunks. Because of the intense sunlight in the tropics, many plants have adapted to living in the canopy. Some of the most common are epiphytes, which are plants that attach themselves to trees. In some forests epiphytes can be very abundant—over 2,000 epiphytes may be found on a single tree.

While the idea of a plant that lives on another plant may seem strange, many house plants are by nature epiphytes. Well-known examples include bromeliads or "air plants" and some kinds of orchids.

Rainforests have a huge variety of tree species. It is not unusual to find more than 200 different types of trees in a couple of acres of rainforest.

Diversity protects species. A species that becomes too abundant in natural forests faces the threat of a predator adapting to exploit its abundance. For example, in the Amazon the failure of rubber tree plantations, where only a single species is grown, is due to a fungus that feeds on the tree. In the natural rainforest, rubber trees are widely dispersed so the fungus can never wipe out more than one individual tree at a time. That's why plantations and single-species agriculture are so susceptible to pests and require toxic chemicals.

Top: Heliconia in the Colombian Amazon; passion vine (Passiflora) flower in Colombia. 2nd row: Tangkoko N.P. in Sulawesi; carnivorous pitcher plant in Borneo; bird nest ferns in Madagascar. 3rd row: Heliconia in Amacayacu N.P., Colombia; Navia tentaculata epiphyte in Venezuela. 4th row: orchid in Torajaland, Sulawesi; sapling in Indonesian Borneo.

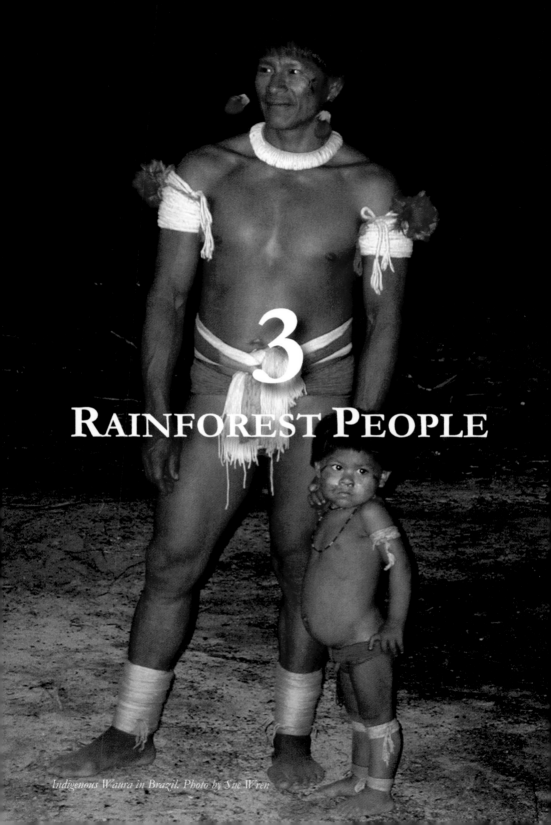

3
RAINFOREST PEOPLE

Indigenous Waura in Brazil. Photo by Sue Wren

A Wauru shaman in the Southern Amazon in Mato Grosso, Brazil. Photo by Sue Wren

One of my first experiences in a "real" rainforest was a visit to an indigenous community in the Ecuadorean Amazon. I was 12 years old at the time and immediately bonded with the kids who were around my age, even though we didn't speak the same language. We spent hours playing in the river and exploring the forest. I had much to learn from them—they had a name for every plant and animal and, most importantly, they knew where to find the coolest lizards, frogs, and insects. They showed me a gigantic stick insect that was nearly as long as my arm and caught a breathtakingly beautiful lizard which looked like a rainbow. They took me to an area of forest where poison dart frogs—like little jewels of color—hopped all around me. It was an experience I will never forget.

Rainforest people

Tropical rainforests are home to tribal peoples who rely on their surroundings for food, shelter, and medicines. Today

Traditional Waura ceremony. Photo by Sue Wren.

very few forest people live in traditional ways; most have been displaced by outside settlers, have been forced to give up their lifestyles by governments, or have chosen to adopt outside customs.

Of the remaining forest people, the Amazon supports the largest native, or indigenous populations, although these people, too, have been impacted by the modern world. While they still depend on the forest for traditional hunting and gathering, most Amerindians, as American indigenous people are called, grow crops (like bananas, manioc, and rice), use western goods (like metal pots, pans, and utensils), and make regular trips to towns and cities to bring foods and wares to market. Still, these forest people can teach us a lot about the rainforest. Their knowledge of medicinal plants used for treating illness is unmatched, and they have a great understanding of the ecology of the Amazon rainforest.

In Africa there are native forest dwellers sometimes known as pygmies. The tallest of these people, also called the Mbuti, rarely exceed 5 feet in height. Their small size enables them to move about the forest more efficiently than taller people.

Great civilizations in the rainforest

Today most forest dwellers live in small settlements or practice nomadic hunting and gathering. In the past, tropical rainforests and surrounding areas supported great civilizations like the Mayas, Incas, and Aztecs that developed complex societies and made important contributions to science.

Machu Pichu in Peru was built by the Inca

Member of the Dani tribe in Indonesian New Guinea

Young Waura in Brazil

These great civilizations faced some of the same environmental problems (excessive forest loss, soil erosion, overpopulation, lack of water supplies) that we face today. For the Maya, the damage they caused to the environment apparently was great enough to cause their downfall.

Medicinal plant knowledge of native people

One of the most exciting areas of research in tropical forests is ethnobotany, which is the study of how people use plants to treat illness and disease. Forest people have an incredible knowledge of medicinal plants, with remedies for everything from snakebites to tumors.

To date, many of the prescription drugs used in the western world have been derived from plants. Seventy percent of the plants identified by the U.S. National Cancer Institute as having anti-cancer characteristics are found only in forests.

The shaman or "medicine man" of a village typically holds

Trio shaman in Suriname (left), and Purko medicineman in Kenya's Loita Hills (right)

knowledge of medicinal plants. The shaman treats the sick, often during elaborate ceremonies and rituals using plants gathered from the surrounding forest.

Shamans have incredible healing powers, but their knowledge is rapidly disappearing as rainforests are cut down and tribes abandon their traditions. Shamans are going extinct faster than rare and endangered species.

What happened to the native people of the Amazon?

Before the beginning of European colonization of the New World in the 15th century, an estimated seven to ten million Amerindians lived in American rainforests, half of them in Brazil. Great cities existed in the Andes, while the Amazon supported agricultural societies.

The arrival of Europeans brought about the end of the native civilizations in Central and South America. Europeans carried diseases that killed millions of Amerindians, and within 100 years of the arrival of these outsiders, the Amerindian population was reduced by 90 percent. Most of the surviving native people lived in the interior of the forest, either pushed there by the Europeans, or living traditionally in smaller groups.

Kids in the rainforest

Although they generally don't watch TV, use the Internet, or play video games, kids in the rainforest do many of the same things you probably do. They play with friends, help their families with chores, and go to school.

Since "rainforest kids" live closer to nature than the average American child, they learn things that are helpful in the environment around them. From an early age many children learn how to fish, hunt, and collect materials and food from the forest. Instead of going to a playground or a shopping mall for fun, children in places like the Amazon spend most of their time outdoors playing in the forest and in rivers and streams.

Wauru boy in Brazil. Photo by Sue Wren

Threats to rainforest people

There are several reasons the lives of forest peoples are changing. Tribes in places like the Amazon and Malaysia are losing their traditional land to governments and developers. The forests they have used for countless generations are being cut down by loggers, torn up by miners, and hunted by poachers. The rivers they use for water and fishing are being dammed to produce electricity for far-off cities. When forest people resist these developments, they may be ridiculed, arrested, forcibly moved, or even killed.

Rainforest people themselves are choosing to change the way they live. For the indigenous, the lure of urban culture is strong. Cities seem to offer the promise of affluence and the conveniences of an easy life. But in leaving their forest homes indigenous peoples usually meet with a stark reality: the skills that serve them so well in the forest don't translate well to an urban setting. The odds are stacked against them; they arrive near the bottom of the social ladder, often not proficient in the language and customs of city dwellers. The lucky ones may find work in factories or as day laborers and security guards, but many eventually return to the countryside. Some re-integrate into their villages, others join the ranks of miners and loggers who trespass on indigenous lands, negotiating deals that pit members of the same tribe against each other in order to exploit the resources they steward. As tribes are fragmented and forests fall, indigenous culture—and its wealth of profound knowledge—is lost. The world is left a poorer place, culturally and biologically.

Top: Orang asli home in Malaysia. Lower left: Purko tribesman in Kenya. Lower right: Dani farmer in the highlands of Papua, Indonesian New Guinea.

4
WHY RAINFORESTS ARE IMPORTANT

Rainforest creek in Belize

Some 2,500 miles (4,000 km) up the Amazon River where it forms the border between Peru, Colombia, and Brazil.

The first time I saw the Amazon river, I was awed by its size. It looked like an ocean; and for good reason.

During the high water season, the Amazon's mouth may be 300 miles wide, and every day up to 17 billion metric tons of water flow into the Atlantic Ocean. For reference, the Amazon discharges enough fresh water daily into the Atlantic to supply New York City's freshwater needs for nine years. The force of the current causes Amazon River water to continue flowing 125 miles out to sea before mixing with Atlantic salt water. Early sailors could drink fresh water out of the ocean before sighting the South American continent.

What is even more awesome about the Amazon is the rainforest that feeds it. Trees are water factories—they release or transpire water into the atmosphere. Across the entire Amazon, trees produce 20 billion tons of water per day, or the equivalent of more than one-fifth of all the fresh water that flows into Earth's oceans!

Why are rainforests important?

Flying over the heart of the Amazon is like flying over an ocean of green: an expanse of trees broken only by rivers. Even more amazing than their size is the role the Amazon and other rainforests around the world play in our everyday lives.

While rainforests may seem like a distant concern, these ecosystems are critically important for our well-being.

Rainforests are often called the lungs of the planet for their role in absorbing carbon dioxide, a greenhouse gas, and producing oxygen, upon which all animals depend for survival. Rainforests also stabilize climate, house incredible amounts of plants and wildlife, and produce nourishing rainfall all around the planet.

Rainforests:
- help stabilize the world's climate;
- provide a home to many plants and animals;
- maintain the water cycle;
- protect against flood, drought, and erosion;
- are a source for medicines and foods;
- support tribal people; and
- are an interesting place to visit.

Rainforests help stabilize climate

Rainforests help stabilize the world's climate by absorbing carbon dioxide from the atmosphere. Scientists have shown that excess carbon dioxide in the atmosphere from human activities is contributing to climate change. Therefore, living rainforests have an

Rainforest in Uganda

important role in mitigating climate change, but when rainforests are chopped down and burned, the carbon stored in their wood and leaves is released into the atmosphere, contributing to climate change.

Rainforests also affect local weather conditions by creating rainfall and moderating temperatures.

Toco Toucan (Ramphastos toco), a toucan found across eastern South America, including the Amazon.

Rainforests provide a home for plants and wildlife

Rainforests are home to a large number of the world's plant and animals species, including many endangered species. As forests are cut down, many species are doomed to extinction.

Most rainforest species can survive only in their natural habitat. As their habitat is destroyed, many well-known rainforest species are threatened with extinction, including orangutans, rhinos, tigers, gorillas, elephants, as well as many birds, monkeys, reptiles, and amphibians.

Zoos cannot save all animals.

Top: Rainforest in Malaysian Borneo; middle left: rainstorm over forest in a deforested region in Brazil; lower left: Iguazu falls in Brazil and Argentina is the product of rainfall generated by the Amazon; right: waterfall in Bwindi National Park, Uganda.

Rainforests help maintain the water cycle

The role of rainforests in the water cycle is to add water to the atmosphere through the process of transpiration (in which plants release water from their leaves during photosynthesis). This moisture contributes to the formation of rain clouds, which release the water back onto the rainforest. In the Amazon, 50-80 percent of moisture remains in the ecosystem's water cycle.

When forests are cut down, less moisture goes into the atmosphere and rainfall declines, sometimes leading to drought.

In recent years, the rainforests of Borneo and the Amazon have experienced very severe droughts. These have been made worse by deforestation.

Moisture generated by rainforests travels around the world. Scientists have discovered that rainfall in America's Midwest is affected by forests in the Congo. Meanwhile, moisture created in the Amazon ends up falling as rain as far away as Texas, and forests in Southeast Asia influence rain patterns in southeastern Europe and China. Distant rainforests are therefore important to farmers everywhere.

Rain approaching over Brazil's Pantanal, a massive freshwater wetland that contains many Amazon species, including tapir and jaguar. The Pantanal is the best place in the world to see jaguar in the wild.

Rainforests reduce erosion

The roots of rainforest trees and vegetation help anchor the soil. When trees are cut down there is no longer anything to protect the ground, and soils are quickly washed away with rain. The process of washing away of soil is known as erosion.

As soil is washed down into rivers it causes problems for fish and people. Fish suffer because water becomes clouded and spawning grounds fill with silt, while people have trouble navigating waterways that are shallower because of the increased amount of dirt in the water. Meanwhile, farmers lose topsoil that is needed for growing crops, and dams generate less electricity.

On steep hillsides, loss of forest can trigger landslides. For example, thousands of people were killed

Erosion on deforested hillsides in Madagascar.

in Central America during Hurricane Mitch of 1998 when deforested hillsides collapsed. Had forests been maintained, the death toll would have been lower.

Forests also play an important role in reducing damage from flooding by reducing the rate of water runoff.

During the devastating 2004 Indian Ocean tsunami, areas where mangrove forests had been cut down suffered more devastation than areas where healthy mangrove forests remained as a buffer. Mangroves also help protect against coastal erosion.

Rainforests provide resources for people

People have long used forests as a source of food, wood, medicine, and recreation. When forests are lost, they can no longer provide these resources. Instead people must find other places to get these goods and services. They also must find ways to pay for the things they once got for free from the forest.

As a frequent visitor to rainforests, I can attest that they provide much more than life-saving medicines and nourishing fruit. Rainforests are found in a variety of landscapes: some are situated on scenic mountain ranges, others hug giant lowland rivers, while more still are found near beautiful beaches and coral reefs. Rainforests offer opportunities for cultural exchange, photography, adventure, fishing, hiking, relaxation, birding and wildlife spotting.

Blue-and-gold macaws flock by the hundreds in parts of the Peruvian Amazon where they gather at clay licks. Manu National Park and Tambopata-Candamo Reserve in southeastern Peru are some of the best places to see wild macaws.

5
DEFORESTATION

Erosion triggered be deforestation in Madagascar

Deforestation in Indonesian Borneo. This area of peat forest was cleared for a rubber plantation.

One of the saddest moments in my life was hearing about the destruction of the tract of rainforest in Borneo described in the introduction. But my work with Mongabay has had happy moments as well, including helping to stop deforestation.

A favorite example comes from Madagascar, that big island off Africa that has lemurs, chameleons, and strange insects. In 2009 there was a military coup in Madagascar, and in the aftermath its beautiful rainforests were logged for a precious timber called rosewood. Because the coup leaders profited from the logging, it was difficult to stop, but given my love for Madagascar, I had to do something, so I started writing articles about what was happening. When I learned that the timber was being trafficked by a European shipping company, I contacted activists, suggesting that now was an opportunity to make the world aware of the situation in Madagascar. Word spread. Tens of thousands of emails went out.

The outcry was so intense, the company stopped shipping rosewood. Global pressure intensified, and within three months, the government of Madagascar banned all shipments of rosewood, slowing down an industry that had been wiping out communities, wildlife, and forests.

Why are rainforests being destroyed?

Every year an area of rainforest the size of New Jersey is cut down and destroyed. The plants and animals that used to live in these forests either die or must find a new forest to call their home. Why are rainforests being destroyed?

Humans are the main cause of rainforest destruction. We are cutting down rainforests for many reasons, including:

- wood for both timber and making fires;
- agriculture for both small and large farms;
- land for poor farmers who don't have anywhere else to live;
- grazing land for cattle;
- pulp for making paper;
- road construction; and
- extraction of minerals and energy.

Peat fires, like this one in Indonesian Borneo, release large amounts of carbon into the atmosphere.

Rainforests are also threatened by climate change, which is contributing to droughts in parts of the Amazon and Southeast Asia. Drought causes die-offs of trees and dries out leaf litter, increasing the risk of forest fires, which are often set by land developers, ranchers, plantation owners, and loggers.

In 2005 and 2010 the Amazon experienced the worst droughts ever recorded. Rivers dried up, isolating communities, and millions of acres burned. The smoke caused widespread health problems, interfered with transportation, and blocked the formation of rain clouds, while the burning contributed huge amounts of carbon dioxide to the atmosphere, worsening the effects of climate change. Meanwhile, Indonesia has experienced several severe droughts in recent decades. The worst occurred in 1982-1983 and 1997-1998 when millions of acres of forest burned.

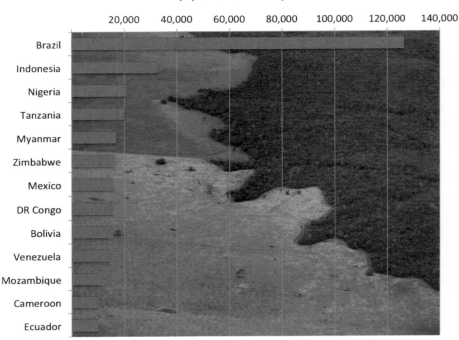

Highest tropical forest loss between 2005 and 2010
(square kilometers)

Logging and timber harvesting in the rainforest

One of the leading causes of rainforest destruction is logging. Many types of wood used for furniture, flooring, and construction are harvested from tropical forests in Africa, Asia, and South America. By buying certain wood products, people in places like the United States and Europe are directly contributing to the destruction of rainforests.

While logging can be carried out in a manner that minimizes damage to the environment, most logging in the rainforest is very destructive. Large trees are cut down and dragged through the forest, while access roads open up remote forest areas to agriculture by poor farmers. In Africa logging workers often rely on "bushmeat" for protein. They hunt wildlife like gorillas, deer, and chimpanzees for food.

Research has found that the number of species found in logged rainforest is much lower than the number found in untouched or "primary" rainforest. Many rainforest animals cannot survive in the changed environment.

Local people often rely on harvesting wood from rainfor-

Lumber cut illegally from forest surrounding Gunung Palung National Park in West Kalimantan, on the island of Borneo. The image on the facing page shows illegal logging within the park.

ests for firewood and building materials. In the past such practices were not particularly damaging to the ecosystem because
there were relatively few people. Today, however, in areas with
large human populations the sheer number of people collect-
ing wood from a rainforest can be extremely damaging. In the
1990s, for example, the forests around the refugee camps in
Central Africa (Rwanda and Congo) were virtually stripped of
all trees in some areas.

Agriculture in the rainforest

Every year thousands of square miles of rainforest are destroyed for agricultural use. The two groups chiefly responsible
for converting rainforest into farmland are poor farmers and
corporations.

Poor farmers in many parts of the world rely on clearing
rainforest to feed their families. Without access to better agricultural lands, these people use slash-and-burn to clear patches
of forest for short-term use. Typically, they farm the cleared
land for a couple of years before the soil is exhausted of nutrients, and they must move on to clear a new patch of forest.

Agricultural companies are clearing more rainforest than ever before, especially in the Amazon where large tracts of rainforest are being converted into soybean farms. Some experts believe that South America will someday have an area of farmland that rivals that of the American Midwest. But much of this farmland will come at the expense of the Amazon rainforest.

In Asia, especially Malaysia and Indonesia, large areas of rainforest are being cleared for oil palm plantations to produce palm oil, which is used widely in processed food, cosmetics, and soap. Today palm oil is found in some 50 percent of packaged snack foods, a proportion that is growing because palm oil is the cheapest type of vegetable oil. Unfortunately, the forests that are being destroyed for palm oil production are home to many endangered species, including orangutans, pygmy elephants, Sumatran tigers, and Javan and Sumatran rhinos.

Deforestation for soybeans in the Brazilian Amazon (left); conversion of rainforest for oil palm on the edge of Gunung Leuser National Park in Sumatra (right). Logged forest and oil palm in Malaysia.

Why are biofuels bad for rainforests?

Recently there has been a lot of interest in using plants to replace fossil fuels like gasoline and diesel that contribute greenhouse gases to the atmosphere, warming the planet.

These plant-based fuels, called biofuels, are typically produced from agricultural crops. There are two main types of biofuels: ethanol and biodiesel. Ethanol is typically made from corn and sugar cane, while biodiesel is made from the fruit of palm trees, soybeans, and canola (also called rapeseed).

Although biofuels produced from agricultural crops can generate less pollution and greenhouse gas emissions than conventional fossil fuels, scientists are finding that most are causing environmental problems. Biofuels may also be hurting the poor. The reason is largely economic.

Now that traditional food crops are being used for the production of energy, there is increased demand for such crops, resulting in higher prices. While higher prices may be good for some farmers who receive more money for the crops they grow, consumers have to pay more for food. In poor countries, where people have very little money, this means that many go hungry. In 2007 and 2008 several countries saw protests and riots by people who could not afford to pay higher prices for food.

Higher prices for crops are also causing other problems. To take advantage of higher prices, farmers all over the world are converting land for crop production. With most of the available land in North America and Europe already used for farming, agriculture is expanding in tropical places, especially in Brazil and Indonesia, where there are still large areas suitable for new agricultural land. The trouble is that some of this land is currently covered by tropical rainforests. When farmers cut down rainforests for farms and ranches, the dead trees release carbon dioxide and other greenhouse gases into the atmo-

New oil palm plantations in Sabah, Malaysia, on the island of Borneo (left); oil palm fruit (right). Vast areas of forest in Indonesia and Malaysia have been converted to oil palm plantations. Amazon rainforest cleared for new soy cultivation in Brazil (below). Landowners in the Brazilian Amazon are required to preserve Brazil nut trees, so they leave these standing but clear the surrounding forest.

sphere (just as when fossil fuels are burned). Furthermore, the destruction of rainforests displaces indigenous people and kills wildlife. Biofuels are thus having a significant impact on the environment.

Some biofuels are less bad than others. When crops are grown on abandoned agriculture lands and in areas that are not covered by natural ecosystems, they can have a low impact on the environment, provided that fertilizers and pesticides are not over-used. In the future, new types of biofuels may produce even fewer greenhouse gas emissions and actually help the environment. For example, the use of native grasses for biofuel production in the United States could offer higher biofuel yields and generate less pollution than corn-based ethanol. At the same time, these grasses can enhance soil fertility and do not drain the water table.

Cattle in the rainforest

Clearing for cattle pasture is the leading cause of deforestation in the Amazon, with Brazil now producing more beef than ever before. Besides raising cattle for food, many landowners

Causes of Deforestation in the Brazilian Amazon, 2000-2005

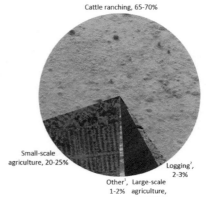

Cattle ranching, 65-70%

Small-scale agriculture, 20-25%

Logging[2], 2-3%

Other[1], 1-2%

Large-scale agriculture, 5-10%

1) Other includes fires, mining, urbanization, road construction, dams;
2) Logging generally results in degradation rather than deforestation, but is often followed by clearing for agriculture.

Cattle and clearing for cattle pasture in the Brazilian Amazon. Most forest cleared in the Amazon ends up as cattle pasture.

use cattle to expand their land holdings. By simply placing cattle on an area of forest land, landowners can gain ownership rights to that land.

Most of the beef produced by Brazil is consumed by Brazilians, but some is exported to overseas markets.

Pulp and paper production from the rainforest

The production of pulp for the paper industry has been one of the biggest causes of deforestation in parts of Indonesia over the past 20 years. Vast areas of rainforest in Sumatra have been logged and converted into fast-growing plantations consisting of only a single species. These plantations are used to produce fiber for wood-pulp and paper, which is turned into cardboard packaging, fast-food wrappers, printer paper, and junk mail. Just think about how much paper we use on a daily basis: paper, in one form or another, comes with almost every product we buy. In some cases that paper is produced directly through the destruction of rainforests.

Consequently, pulp and paper production is now one of the biggest threats to the critically endangered Sumatran tiger.

Rainforest cleared for rubber trees in Laos. Chinese and Vietnamese companies are converting large areas of forest in Laos for plantations since both countries have little forest available.

Road construction in the rainforest

Road and highway construction in the rainforest opens up large areas to deforestation. In Brazil, the Trans-Amazonian highway resulted in the destruction of huge areas of forest by colonists, loggers, and land speculators. In Africa, logging roads give access to poachers who hunt endangered wildlife as "bushmeat" or meat sold to city dwellers. Some of the poached wildlife—especially rhinos, pangolin, and tigers—goes to Asia where it is used for traditional Chinese medicine.

Therefore it is very important that when new roads are built in rainforest areas, they are carefully planned to minimize the environmental impacts. One way to reduce deforestation from road construction is to create protected areas on either side of the road.

Extraction of minerals and energy from the rainforest

Gold, copper, diamonds, and other precious metals and gemstones are important resources that are found in rainforests around the world. Extracting these natural resources is frequently a destructive activity that damages the rainforest ecosystem and causes problems for people living nearby and downstream from mining operations, especially from toxic run-off into river systems. There have been cases of mining companies—sometimes working with local police or authorities—forcibly displacing forest people from their lands in order to exploit mineral riches. Examples are gold mining in the Brazilian and Peruvian Amazon, rare earth mining in the Congo, and gold and copper mining in Indonesia and Papua New Guinea.

Some of the world's most promising oil and gas deposits lie deep in tropical rainforests. Unfortunately oil and gas development often takes a heavy toll on the environment and local people. Oil and gas development in rainforest areas causes displacement of local people, air and water pollution,

A large gold mine in the Peruvian Amazon (top). The cleared area was once a river surrounded by rainforest. Roads in Indonesian Borneo (left) and New Guinea (right). Rainforest roads provide access to loggers, commercial hunters, and colonists.

deforestation, and construction of roads that open previously inaccessible areas to deforestation. High energy prices in recent years have spurred increased exploration of rainforests for oil and gas. The western Amazon—including Colombia, Ecuador, Peru, and Brazil—has seen a lot of activity. More than 70 percent of the Peruvian Amazon—including indigenous territories and conservation areas—is now under concession for oil and gas.

Dams are also a big threat to rainforests, particularly in the Amazon, the Mekong (Laos and Burma or Myanmar), and Malaysia. Dams disrupt river systems, flood rainforest, displace forest people, and support activities that cause more deforestation. In Sarawak, which is part of Malaysian Borneo, more than a dozen dams are being planned. These will force thousands of forest-dependent people to move and will inundate important rainforest areas. The power generated by the dams will be used for large-scale mining activities, causing further destruction. Similarly, in Brazil, Belo Monte dam will block the Xingu river, a tributary of the Amazon, flooding more than 100,000 acres of rainforest and displacing more than 15,000 people. Electricity from the project will power mining activities and industrial agriculture that will destroy yet more rainforest. Indigenous people, scientists, and environmentalists strongly oppose the project.

The role of poverty in deforestation

Poverty plays a major role in deforestation. The world's rainforests are found in the poorest areas on the planet. The people who live in and around rainforests rely on these ecosystems for their survival. They collect fruit and wood, hunt wildlife to put meat on the table, and are paid by companies that extract re-

Impoverished children in Western Madagascar.

Kids in Indonesian New Guinea

sources from forest lands.

Most rural poor never have the options that we in Western countries take for granted. These people almost never have a choice to go to college or become a doctor, factory worker, or secretary. They must live off the land that surrounds them and make use of whatever resources they can find. Their poverty costs the entire world through the loss of tropical rainforests and wildlife. Without providing for these people, rainforests cannot be saved.

However, people in the wealthier world, such as the U.S. and Europe, also play a large role in the destruction of rainforests, even if the forests are very far away.

Population and consumption

The underlying cause of most environmental problems is human population and over-consumption: both the population in the temperate region that relies on resources derived from tropical rainforests, and the expanding population of developing tropical nations, who exploit the rainforest for survival.

While it may seem hard to believe, people in rich countries

Logging truck in Malaysian Borneo

like the United States have a disproportionate impact on the environment through our consumption patterns. We use far more resources than poor farmers in tropical countries. For example, the food we buy in grocery stores may be produced through deforestation for soy in the Amazon or palm oil in Indonesia. The materials and energy to build and power our mobile phones and laptops may come from the destruction of rainforests in the Congo and Colombia. The paper we use for printing, packaging, hygiene products and the books we read may be produced from the logging of rainforests in Indonesia. Only by reducing our environmental footprint at home can we ever hope to save rainforests and other wilderness areas.

Overpopulation is a major concern. As more people are added to the planet, there are fewer resources to share. Crowded conditions and scarcity of resources often lead to conflict or other problems. Animals lose habitat to cities and expanding farm lands.

6
SAVING RAINFORESTS

Sumatran orangutans in Gunung Palung National Park, Indonesia

Deforestation in Indonesian Borneo. This area of peat forest was cleared for an oil palm plantation.

In the tiny South American country of Suriname I saw something amazing: tribesmen dressed only in loincloths using 21st century technology to map their rainforest lands.

The Trio, as the Indian tribe is known, were using handheld GPS units to mark details of their forest homeland, including the location of creeks, sites where medicinal plants are located, and places of spiritual value. The data collected were assembled into a map which the tribe used to prove to the government that it "used" the land. The Trio hoped the map would convince the government to grant it official rights to the land.

The Trio also regularly used Google Earth to monitor its territory for illegal logging and mining. If they detected deforestation, the Trio reported it to authorities. The Trio illustrate some of the exciting new approaches being used to save rainforests around the world.

How can we save rainforests?

Rainforests are disappearing very quickly. The good news is there are a lot of people who want to save rainforests. The bad news is that saving rainforests is not going to be easy. It will take the efforts of many people working together in order to ensure that rainforests and their wildlife will survive for your children to appreciate, enjoy, and benefit from.

Some steps for saving rainforests and, on a broader scale, ecosystems around the world can be abbreviated as TREES:

- Teach others about the importance of the environment and how they can help save rainforests.
- Restore damaged ecosystems by planting trees on land where forests have been cut down.
- Encourage people to live in a way that doesn't hurt the environment
- Establish parks to protect rainforests and wildlife
- Support companies that operate in ways that minimize damage to the environment

Saving rainforests through education

Education is a critical part of saving the world's rainforests. People must see the beauty and understand the importance of these forests so they will want to protect them. Environmental education should occur both in western countries like the United States and in countries like Bolivia and Madagascar that have rainforests.

In the United States, people need to understand their role in the loss of rainforests. For example, buying certain products like mahogany contributes to the cutting down of rainforests in other countries. If we make an effort to learn about the environment, we can understand what we're losing as rainforest disappears. We can also make decisions to buy products and support companies and organizations that help the rainforest.

In rainforest countries, local people sometimes do not know

Indigenous guide in Peru

why forests are important. Through educational programs these people can learn that forests provide key services (like clean water) and are home to plants and animals found nowhere else in the world. Few children in Madagascar know that lemurs are not found in America. They are proud and happy when they learn that lemurs only live in Madagascar.

In other cases, however, people already know that forests are important. Where they need help is in fighting companies that are taking their land and destroying rainforests.

In some tropical countries, governments may not fully recognize the rights of forest people. Instead, governments may sell forest lands to companies that chop down trees for timber or industrial agriculture. Local people therefore need help learning about legal processes so they can defend forest lands against destructive companies.

The Internet, mobile phones, and satellite monitoring have created new opportunities for communities to mobilize against forest·destruction. Tools like Facebook and Twitter can help

With the support of the Amazon Conservation Team, Google, and other organizations, tribes in the Amazon are now using cutting-edge technology to map, monitor, and protect their territories from illegal loggers and miners. The image in the upper left shows the Surui indigenous territory in Brazil, which the Surui have now mapped. Their map includes rivers and creeks as well as places of spiritual significance, areas rich with medicinal plants, and hunting grounds. The region around the Surui territory has been largely deforested, demonstrating the role indigenous people can play in protecting forests. As Mark Plotkin, founder and president of the Amazon Conservation Team says: "If you are an illegal logger, where would you rather operate: a national park with no guards or an area of forest full of people heavily armed with spears and poison-tipped arrows?"

Bottom photo by Fernando Bizerra, BG Press, courtesy of the Amazon Conservation Team people organize campaigns and protests when their rights are being ignored or violated. Google Earth is helping scientists, environmentalists, and even indigenous people see where forests are threatened by logging and mining.

Finally, education is important for improving people's quality of life. One of the most effective ways to reduce population growth and alleviate poverty is through education, especially education of girls and young women.

Reforestation in Sulawesi

Rehabilitate and restore rainforests

In trying to protect rainforests, we also need to look at how damaged forests can be brought back to health. While it is impossible to replant a rainforest, some rainforests can recover after they have been cut down—especially if natural forests remain nearby or they have some help through the planting of trees. In some cases it is also possible to use deforested lands for improved forms of agriculture to provide food for people living nearby. When these people have enough food, they will not need to cut down more forest to plant crops.

One promising area of research looks at ancient societies

that lived in the Amazon rainforest before the arrival of Europeans in the 15th century. Apparently these populations were able to enrich the rainforest soil, which is usually quite poor, using charcoal and animal bones. By improving soil quality, large areas of the Amazon that have already been deforested could be used to support agriculture. This could reduce pressure on rainforest areas for agricultural land. Further, the "terra preta" soil as it's called, could help fight climate change since it absorbs carbon dioxide, an important greenhouse gas.

Encourage people to live in ways that do not hurt the environment

A key part of saving rainforests and the environment is encouraging all people to live in ways that do less harm to the world around them. Driving less, using fuel efficient cars and public transport, conserving water, recycling, and turning off lights when you don't need them are all ways that you and your family can reduce your impact on the environment.

In rainforest countries many scientists and organizations are working to help local people live in ways that cause less damage to the environment. Some people call this idea "sustainable development." Sustainable development has a goal of improving the lives of people while at the same time protecting the environment. Without improving the livelihoods of people living in and around rainforests, it is very difficult to protect parks and wildlife. Conservation must be in the interest of local people to make parks work.

Establish parks that protect rainforests and wildlife

Creating protected areas like national parks is a great way to save rainforests and other ecosystems. Protected areas are locations preserved because of their environmental or cultural value. Generally, protected areas are managed by governments and use park rangers and guards to enforce the rules of the

Strangler fig (Ficus sp.) in Sulawesi

park and protect against illegal activities like hunting, mining, and the cutting down of trees.

Today, parks protect many of the world's most endangered species. Animals like Pandas are found only in protected areas.

Parks are most successful when they have the support of local people living in and around the protected area. If local people have an interest in the park they may form a "community watch" to protect the park from illegal logging and wildlife poaching.

An effective way to protect rainforests is to involve indigenous people in park management. Indigenous people know more about the forest than anyone and have an interest in safeguarding it as a productive ecosystem that provides them food, shelter, and clean water. Research has found that in some cases, "indigenous reserves" may actually protect rainforest better than "national parks" in the Amazon.

Parks can also help the economy in rainforest countries by attracting foreign tourists who pay entrance fees, hire local wilderness guides, and buy local handicrafts like baskets, T-shirts, and beaded bracelets.

Support companies that don't hurt the environment

Today, some companies are concerned about the environment. These companies look for ways to reduce their impact on the world around them through recycling, using less energy, and supporting conservation efforts in other countries. If consumers like you and your parents support these companies by buying their products and services, the environment will be better off.

One way to learn what companies have responsible practices is to ask a local environmental group or do research online. Beware that some companies try to mislead people about their environmental record. It's best to seek independent opinions on the environmental practices of a company rather than relying solely on what a company states on its own web site.

Another way to learn which companies are making efforts to reduce their environmental impact is to check whether their products have been eco-certified, which means that an independent group has evaluated the environmental impact of its products. Examples of eco-certification initiatives are the Forest Stewardship Council (FSC) for wood products, the Roundtable on Sustainable Palm Oil (RSPO) for palm oil, and the Rainforest Alliance for other products. None of these systems are perfect, but they are often better than the alternative: non-certified products. Be sure to do a little research about eco-certification, because sometimes companies use fake certification systems.

Ecotourism

Ecotourism is environmentally responsible travel to enjoy and appreciate nature and cultural experiences. Ecotourism should have low impact on the environment and should contribute to the well-being of local people.

Rangers tracking gorillas in Bwindi, Uganda

What you do can at home to help the environment

There are several things you can do at home to help reduce your impact on the environment.

• Eat less beef and pork. Fish (check Seafood Watch from the Monterey Bay Aquarium to see what types are ok) and poultry have a much lower impact on the environment, while other protein sources such as nuts and organic soy are even less damaging to the planet.

• Think about packaging before you buy products. Individually-wrapped candy uses resources and generates a lot of trash, while fruits and vegetables are healthier and mean less waste.

• Turn off lights and other electrical devices when you don't need them. When light bulbs burn out, replace them with energy-efficient bulbs.

• Do not waste water.

• Recycle.

• Encourage your parents to drive fuel-efficient cars and not to overheat their house.

• Don't let your pets go when you don't want them any more. Feral pets can have a destructive impact on the local environment. Before buying a pet be sure that you are ready to take care of it. Having a pet is a responsibility.

• Think about where the things you buy come from and how they are made. Sometimes it's better not to buy something new, and buy it used instead. Or skip buying it altogether if it's not necessary.

• Get involved! Join a local environmental group that is working to make a difference. For example, Mongabay has selected the following organizations as recipients of its annual conservation award, which recognizes groups that are using innovative methods for protecting forests, oceans, and other ecosystems: the Amazon Conservation Team, for its work with indigenous tribes in trying to protect the

Amazon; Health in Harmony, which is helping protect rainforests in Borneo by providing health care to local communities; and WildlifeDirect, which has created a system for funding park rangers and other conservation workers at dozens of sites around the world.

• Tell your family, friends, and relatives that you want to do more to protect the environment and why it's important to do so. Spreading the word is very important.

Things you can do to help save rainforests:

• Don't buy products made from wildlife skins.
• Don't buy exotic pets that have been collected from the wild. You can ask pet stores whether animals are "wild-caught" or "captive bred." "Captive bred" animals are more friendly for the environment.
• Buy recycled paper.
• Don't buy wood products from Indonesia, Malaysia, Brazil, or Africa unless you know they come from eco-friendly suppliers. A good way to know if wood is rainforest-safe is if it has a "certification label." An example of a certification label is "FSC-certified" which means the wood comes from sustainably managed forests.
• Learn more about rainforests and the plants and animals that live in them. Tell your friends and parents why rainforests are important.
• Join an organization or an Internet group (Facebook has many communities) that is working to protect rainforests or wildlife.

RESOURCES

The Internet is full of resources for learning more about tropical rainforests and other ecosystems. Here are a few sites where you can start.

Rainforests
- Mongabay-Rainforests (rainforests.mongabay.com)
- Canopy In The Clouds (www.canopyintheclouds.com)
- ACEER (www.wcupa.edu/aceer)
- Forests.org (forests.org)

Environment
- Mongabay (www.mongabay.com)
- Wilderness Classroom (www.wildernessclassroom.com)
- The Wild Classroom (www.thewildclassroom.com)
- NOVA (www.pbs.org/wgbh/nova/)
- Yale Environment 360 (e360.yale.edu/)
- TreeHugger (www.treehugger.com)
- Grist (www.grist.org)
- The Guardian (www.guardian.co.uk/environment)
- National Geographic (www.nationalgeographic.com)

Mongabay.com is widely acknowledged one of the top sources for up-to-date news and information on tropical rainforests, conservation, and environmental issues, so it is a great place to start your exploration.

A web version of *Rainforests* is available in nearly 40 languages at world.mongabay.com

ACKNOWLEDGMENTS

Thank you to Jeremy Hance, Nancy Butler, Alyson Blume, and Carol Van Strum for copy-editing and helpful suggestions on *Rainforests*.

Rainforests and mongabay.com would not have been possible without the love and support of my family.

ABOUT THE AUTHOR

Rhett Butler founded mongabay.com in 1999 and runs the web site full-time. He lives in the San Francisco Bay Area and frequently travels to rainforests around the world.